VEGETABLE G

Seed Starting • Transplar
Growing Under Cover • Fertilizers • Pest Control
Harvest Notes • Observations

Simple Start Guides
Everett, WA

VEGETABLE GARDENING

Seed Starting • Transplanting • Soil Preparation
Growing Under Cover • Fertilizers • Pest Control
Harvest Notes • Observations

Created by Simple Start Guides
Everett, WA 98201

For permissions contact:
SimpleStartGuides@gmail.com

Cover Photo by Cindy L Shebley
Used with Permission

Interior Photos by Cindy L Shebley
Used with permission

ISBN: 9781093421613

SEED STARTING

JOURNAL

Plant Name
Botanical Name

Date Started
Packet Size

Water
Requirements
💧 💧💧 💧💧💧

Sunlight ☀ ◑ ●

☐ Seed ☐ Start ☐ Cutting ☐ Fruit Tree/Bush ☐ Rooting Hormone
☐ Division ☐ Seed Potato ☐ Seed Garlic ☐ Certified Organic ☐ Inoculant

Date	Event

Notes ☐ Gro-Lights ☐ Thinning ☐ Potting On ☐ Hardening Off ☐ Cold Frame

Planting Medium Damping Off Problems? ☐ Yes ☐ No

Fertilizers ☐ Organic ☐ Liquid ☐ Time-Release

Germination Rate ☐ Poor ☐ Average ☐ Good ☐ Excellent

Seed Company _____ Price:_____

Plant Name	Date Started
Botanical Name	**Packet Size**

Water Requirements 💧 💧💧 💧💧💧   Sunlight ☀ ⛅ ●

☐ Seed ☐ Start ☐ Cutting ☐ Fruit Tree/Bush ☐ Rooting Hormone

☐ Division ☐ Seed Potato ☐ Seed Garlic ☐ Certified Organic ☐ Inoculant

Date	Event

Notes ☐ Gro-Lights ☐ Thinning ☐ Potting On ☐ Hardening Off ☐ Cold Frame

Planting Medium   Damping Off Problems? ☐ Yes ☐ No

Fertilizers   ☐ Organic ☐ Liquid ☐ Time-Release

Germination Rate   ☐ Poor ☐ Average ☐ Good ☐ Excellent

Seed Company _____   Price:_____

Plant Name
Botanical Name

Date Started
Packet Size

Water
Requirements   💧   💧💧   💧💧💧   Sunlight   ☀   ☼   ⬤

- ☐ Seed
- ☐ Division
- ☐ Start
- ☐ Seed Potato
- ☐ Cutting
- ☐ Seed Garlic
- ☐ Fruit Tree/Bush
- ☐ Certified Organic
- ☐ Rooting Hormone
- ☐ Inoculant

Date	Event

Notes   ☐ Gro-Lights   ☐ Thinning   ☐ Potting On   ☐ Hardening Off   ☐ Cold Frame

Planting Medium   Damping Off Problems? ☐ Yes ☐ No

Fertilizers   ☐ Organic   ☐ Liquid   ☐ Time-Release

Germination Rate   ☐ Poor   ☐ Average   ☐ Good   ☐ Excellent

Seed Company _____   Price:_____

Plant Name
Botanical Name

Date Started
Packet Size

Water Requirements 💧 💧💧 💧💧💧   Sunlight ☀ ◐ ●

- ☐ Seed
- ☐ Division
- ☐ Start
- ☐ Seed Potato
- ☐ Cutting
- ☐ Seed Garlic
- ☐ Fruit Tree/Bush
- ☐ Certified Organic
- ☐ Rooting Hormone
- ☐ Inoculant

Date	Event

Notes   ☐ Gro-Lights ☐ Thinning ☐ Potting On ☐ Hardening Off ☐ Cold Frame

Planting Medium   Damping Off Problems? ☐ Yes ☐ No

Fertilizers   ☐ Organic ☐ Liquid ☐ Time-Release

Germination Rate   ☐ Poor ☐ Average ☐ Good ☐ Excellent

Seed Company _____   Price:_____

Plant Name	**Date Started**
Botanical Name	**Packet Size**

Water Requirements 💧 💧💧 💧💧💧   Sunlight ☀ ☀ ⬤

- ☐ Seed ☐ Start ☐ Cutting ☐ Fruit Tree/Bush ☐ Rooting Hormone
- ☐ Division ☐ Seed Potato ☐ Seed Garlic ☐ Certified Organic ☐ Inoculant

Date	Event

Notes   ☐ Gro-Lights ☐ Thinning ☐ Potting On ☐ Hardening Off ☐ Cold Frame

Planting Medium   Damping Off Problems? ☐ Yes ☐ No

Fertilizers   ☐ Organic ☐ Liquid ☐ Time-Release

Germination Rate   ☐ Poor ☐ Average ☐ Good ☐ Excellent

Seed Company _____ Price:_____

Plant Name
Botanical Name

Date Started
Packet Size

Water Requirements 🌢 🌢🌢 🌢🌢🌢   Sunlight ☀ ◐ ⬤

- [ ] Seed
- [ ] Division
- [ ] Start
- [ ] Seed Potato
- [ ] Cutting
- [ ] Seed Garlic
- [ ] Fruit Tree/Bush
- [ ] Certified Organic
- [ ] Rooting Hormone
- [ ] Inoculant

Date	Event

Notes   [ ] Gro-Lights [ ] Thinning [ ] Potting On [ ] Hardening Off [ ] Cold Frame

Planting Medium   Damping Off Problems? [ ] Yes [ ] No

Fertilizers   [ ] Organic [ ] Liquid [ ] Time-Release

Germination Rate   [ ] Poor [ ] Average [ ] Good [ ] Excellent

Seed Company _____ Price:_____

Plant Name	Date Started
Botanical Name	Packet Size

Water Requirements 💧 💧💧 💧💧💧   Sunlight ☀ ◐ ●

- ☐ Seed
- ☐ Division
- ☐ Start
- ☐ Seed Potato
- ☐ Cutting
- ☐ Seed Garlic
- ☐ Fruit Tree/Bush
- ☐ Certified Organic
- ☐ Rooting Hormone
- ☐ Inoculant

Date	Event

Notes   ☐ Gro-Lights ☐ Thinning ☐ Potting On ☐ Hardening Off ☐ Cold Frame

Planting Medium   Damping Off Problems? ☐ Yes ☐ No

Fertilizers   ☐ Organic ☐ Liquid ☐ Time-Release

Germination Rate   ☐ Poor ☐ Average ☐ Good ☐ Excellent

Seed Company _____   Price:_____

Plant Name
Botanical Name

Date Started
Packet Size

Water Requirements 💧 💧💧 💧💧💧

Sunlight ☀ ◐ ●

☐ Seed ☐ Start ☐ Cutting ☐ Fruit Tree/Bush ☐ Rooting Hormone

☐ Division ☐ Seed Potato ☐ Seed Garlic ☐ Certified Organic ☐ Inoculant

Date	Event

Notes ☐ Gro-Lights ☐ Thinning ☐ Potting On ☐ Hardening Off ☐ Cold Frame

Planting Medium   Damping Off Problems? ☐ Yes ☐ No

Fertilizers   ☐ Organic ☐ Liquid ☐ Time-Release

Germination Rate   ☐ Poor ☐ Average ☐ Good ☐ Excellent

Seed Company _____ Price:_____

Plant Name
Botanical Name

Date Started
Packet Size

Water Requirements 💧 💧💧 💧💧💧

Sunlight ☀ ☼ ●

- ☐ Seed
- ☐ Division
- ☐ Start
- ☐ Seed Potato
- ☐ Cutting
- ☐ Seed Garlic
- ☐ Fruit Tree/Bush
- ☐ Certified Organic
- ☐ Rooting Hormone
- ☐ Inoculant

Date	Event

Notes ☐ Gro-Lights ☐ Thinning ☐ Potting On ☐ Hardening Off ☐ Cold Frame

Planting Medium Damping Off Problems? ☐ Yes ☐ No

Fertilizers ☐ Organic ☐ Liquid ☐ Time-Release

Germination Rate ☐ Poor ☐ Average ☐ Good ☐ Excellent

Seed Company _____ Price:_____

| Plant Name | Date Started |
| Botanical Name | Packet Size |

Water Requirements 💧 💧💧 💧💧💧   Sunlight ☀ ☀ ⬤

- ☐ Seed
- ☐ Division
- ☐ Start
- ☐ Seed Potato
- ☐ Cutting
- ☐ Seed Garlic
- ☐ Fruit Tree/Bush
- ☐ Certified Organic
- ☐ Rooting Hormone
- ☐ Inoculant

Date	Event

Notes   ☐ Gro-Lights ☐ Thinning ☐ Potting On ☐ Hardening Off ☐ Cold Frame

Planting Medium   Damping Off Problems? ☐ Yes ☐ No

Fertilizers   ☐ Organic ☐ Liquid ☐ Time-Release

Germination Rate   ☐ Poor ☐ Average ☐ Good ☐ Excellent

Seed Company _____   Price:_____

| **Plant Name** | **Date Started** |
| **Botanical Name** | **Packet Size** |

Water Requirements 💧 💧💧 💧💧💧   Sunlight ☀ ◐ ●

☐ Seed ☐ Start ☐ Cutting ☐ Fruit Tree/Bush ☐ Rooting Hormone
☐ Division ☐ Seed Potato ☐ Seed Garlic ☐ Certified Organic ☐ Inoculant

Date	Event

Notes ☐ Gro-Lights ☐ Thinning ☐ Potting On ☐ Hardening Off ☐ Cold Frame

Planting Medium   Damping Off Problems? ☐ Yes ☐ No

Fertilizers   ☐ Organic ☐ Liquid ☐ Time-Release

Germination Rate   ☐ Poor ☐ Average ☐ Good ☐ Excellent

Seed Company _____   Price:_____

Plant Name
Botanical Name

Date Started
Packet Size

Water
Requirements 🌢 🌢🌢 🌢🌢🌢   Sunlight ☀ ◑ ●

☐ Seed ☐ Start ☐ Cutting ☐ Fruit Tree/Bush ☐ Rooting Hormone
☐ Division ☐ Seed Potato ☐ Seed Garlic ☐ Certified Organic ☐ Inoculant

Date	Event

Notes ☐ Gro-Lights ☐ Thinning ☐ Potting On ☐ Hardening Off ☐ Cold Frame

Planting Medium   Damping Off Problems? ☐ Yes ☐ No

Fertilizers   ☐ Organic ☐ Liquid ☐ Time-Release

Germination Rate   ☐ Poor ☐ Average ☐ Good ☐ Excellent

Seed Company _____   Price:_____

Plant Name
Botanical Name

Date Started
Packet Size

Water
Requirements 💧 💧💧 💧💧💧   Sunlight ☼ ◐ ●

☐ Seed   ☐ Start   ☐ Cutting   ☐ Fruit Tree/Bush   ☐ Rooting Hormone
☐ Division   ☐ Seed Potato   ☐ Seed Garlic   ☐ Certified Organic   ☐ Inoculant

Date	Event

Notes   ☐ Gro-Lights ☐ Thinning ☐ Potting On ☐ Hardening Off ☐ Cold Frame

Planting Medium   Damping Off Problems? ☐ Yes ☐ No

Fertilizers   ☐ Organic ☐ Liquid ☐ Time-Release

Germination Rate   ☐ Poor ☐ Average ☐ Good ☐ Excellent

Seed Company _____   Price:_____

Plant Name
Botanical Name

Date Started
Packet Size

Water
Requirements 💧 💧💧 💧💧💧   Sunlight ☀ ◐ ●

- ☐ Seed
- ☐ Division
- ☐ Start
- ☐ Seed Potato
- ☐ Cutting
- ☐ Seed Garlic
- ☐ Fruit Tree/Bush
- ☐ Certified Organic
- ☐ Rooting Hormone
- ☐ Inoculant

Date	Event

Notes   ☐ Gro-Lights ☐ Thinning ☐ Potting On ☐ Hardening Off ☐ Cold Frame

Planting Medium   Damping Off Problems? ☐ Yes ☐ No

Fertilizers   ☐ Organic ☐ Liquid ☐ Time-Release

Germination Rate   ☐ Poor ☐ Average ☐ Good ☐ Excellent

Seed Company _____ Price:_____

Plant Name
Botanical Name

Date Started
Packet Size

Water Requirements   💧   💧💧   💧💧💧   Sunlight ☀ ◑ ●

☐ Seed   ☐ Start   ☐ Cutting   ☐ Fruit Tree/Bush   ☐ Rooting Hormone

☐ Division   ☐ Seed Potato   ☐ Seed Garlic   ☐ Certified Organic   ☐ Inoculant

Date	Event

Notes   ☐ Gro-Lights   ☐ Thinning   ☐ Potting On   ☐ Hardening Off   ☐ Cold Frame

Planting Medium   Damping Off Problems? ☐ Yes   ☐ No

Fertilizers   ☐ Organic   ☐ Liquid   ☐ Time-Release

Germination Rate   ☐ Poor   ☐ Average   ☐ Good   ☐ Excellent

Seed Company _____   Price:_____

Plant Name

Botanical Name

Date Started

Packet Size

Water
Requirements 💧 💧💧 💧💧💧   Sunlight ☀ ◑ ⬤

- ☐ Seed
- ☐ Division
- ☐ Start
- ☐ Seed Potato
- ☐ Cutting
- ☐ Seed Garlic
- ☐ Fruit Tree/Bush
- ☐ Certified Organic
- ☐ Rooting Hormone
- ☐ Inoculant

Date	Event

Notes   ☐ Gro-Lights ☐ Thinning ☐ Potting On ☐ Hardening Off ☐ Cold Frame

Planting Medium   Damping Off Problems? ☐ Yes ☐ No

Fertilizers   ☐ Organic   ☐ Liquid   ☐ Time-Release

Germination Rate   ☐ Poor ☐ Average ☐ Good ☐ Excellent

Seed Company _____   Price:_____

Plant Name
Botanical Name

Date Started
Packet Size

Water
Requirements 💧 💧💧 💧💧💧

Sunlight ☀ 🌓 ⬤

- ☐ Seed
- ☐ Division
- ☐ Start
- ☐ Seed Potato
- ☐ Cutting
- ☐ Seed Garlic
- ☐ Fruit Tree/Bush
- ☐ Certified Organic
- ☐ Rooting Hormone
- ☐ Inoculant

Date	Event

Notes   ☐ Gro-Lights ☐ Thinning ☐ Potting On ☐ Hardening Off ☐ Cold Frame

Planting Medium   Damping Off Problems? ☐ Yes ☐ No

Fertilizers   ☐ Organic ☐ Liquid ☐ Time-Release

Germination Rate   ☐ Poor ☐ Average ☐ Good ☐ Excellent

Seed Company _____   Price:_____

Plant Name
Botanical Name

Date Started
Packet Size

Water
Requirements ● ●● ●●●   Sunlight ☼ ◑ ●

- [ ] Seed   - [ ] Start   - [ ] Cutting   - [ ] Fruit Tree/Bush   - [ ] Rooting Hormone
- [ ] Division   - [ ] Seed Potato   - [ ] Seed Garlic   - [ ] Certified Organic   - [ ] Inoculant

Date	Event

Notes   - [ ] Gro-Lights - [ ] Thinning - [ ] Potting On - [ ] Hardening Off - [ ] Cold Frame

Planting Medium   Damping Off Problems? - [ ] Yes - [ ] No

Fertilizers   - [ ] Organic - [ ] Liquid - [ ] Time-Release

Germination Rate   - [ ] Poor - [ ] Average - [ ] Good - [ ] Excellent

Seed Company _____   Price:_____

Plant Name
Botanical Name

Date Started
Packet Size

Water
Requirements   💧 💧💧 💧💧💧   Sunlight   ☀ ◐ ●

☐ Seed   ☐ Start   ☐ Cutting   ☐ Fruit Tree/Bush   ☐ Rooting Hormone
☐ Division   ☐ Seed Potato ☐ Seed Garlic   ☐ Certified Organic ☐ Inoculant

Date	Event

Notes   ☐ Gro-Lights ☐ Thinning ☐ Potting On ☐ Hardening Off ☐ Cold Frame

Planting Medium   Damping Off Problems? ☐ Yes ☐ No

Fertilizers   ☐ Organic ☐ Liquid ☐ Time-Release

Germination Rate   ☐ Poor ☐ Average ☐ Good ☐ Excellent

Seed Company _____   Price:_____

Plant Name

Botanical Name

Date Started

Packet Size

Water Requirements 💧 💧💧 💧💧💧   Sunlight ☀ ◐ ●

☐ Seed   ☐ Start   ☐ Cutting   ☐ Fruit Tree/Bush   ☐ Rooting Hormone

☐ Division   ☐ Seed Potato   ☐ Seed Garlic   ☐ Certified Organic   ☐ Inoculant

Date	Event

Notes   ☐ Gro-Lights ☐ Thinning ☐ Potting On ☐ Hardening Off ☐ Cold Frame

Planting Medium   Damping Off Problems? ☐ Yes ☐ No

Fertilizers   ☐ Organic ☐ Liquid ☐ Time-Release

Germination Rate   ☐ Poor ☐ Average ☐ Good ☐ Excellent

Seed Company _____   Price:_____

Plant Name
Botanical Name

Date Started
Packet Size

Water
Requirements 🌢 🌢🌢 🌢🌢🌢   Sunlight ☀ ◑ ⬤

☐ Seed   ☐ Start   ☐ Cutting   ☐ Fruit Tree/Bush   ☐ Rooting Hormone
☐ Division ☐ Seed Potato ☐ Seed Garlic ☐ Certified Organic ☐ Inoculant

Date	Event

Notes   ☐ Gro-Lights ☐ Thinning ☐ Potting On ☐ Hardening Off ☐ Cold Frame

Planting Medium   Damping Off Problems? ☐ Yes ☐ No

Fertilizers   ☐ Organic ☐ Liquid ☐ Time-Release

Germination Rate   ☐ Poor ☐ Average ☐ Good ☐ Excellent

Seed Company _____   Price:_____

Plant Name
Botanical Name

Date Started
Packet Size

Water
Requirements   💧   💧💧   💧💧💧   Sunlight   ☀   ◐   ●

☐ Seed   ☐ Start   ☐ Cutting   ☐ Fruit Tree/Bush   ☐ Rooting Hormone
☐ Division   ☐ Seed Potato ☐ Seed Garlic   ☐ Certified Organic   ☐ Inoculant

Date	Event

Notes   ☐ Gro-Lights ☐ Thinning ☐ Potting On ☐ Hardening Off ☐ Cold Frame

Planting Medium   Damping Off Problems? ☐ Yes ☐ No

Fertilizers   ☐ Organic ☐ Liquid ☐ Time-Release

Germination Rate   ☐ Poor ☐ Average ☐ Good ☐ Excellent

Seed Company _____   Price:_____

Plant Name
Botanical Name

Date Started
Packet Size

Water
Requirements 💧 💧💧 💧💧💧

Sunlight ☀ 🌤 ●

- [ ] Seed
- [ ] Division
- [ ] Start
- [ ] Seed Potato
- [ ] Cutting
- [ ] Seed Garlic
- [ ] Fruit Tree/Bush
- [ ] Certified Organic
- [ ] Rooting Hormone
- [ ] Inoculant

Date	Event

Notes   - [ ] Gro-Lights - [ ] Thinning - [ ] Potting On - [ ] Hardening Off - [ ] Cold Frame

Planting Medium   Damping Off Problems? - [ ] Yes - [ ] No

Fertilizers   - [ ] Organic - [ ] Liquid - [ ] Time-Release

Germination Rate   - [ ] Poor - [ ] Average - [ ] Good - [ ] Excellent

Seed Company _____   Price:_____

Plant Name
Botanical Name

Date Started
Packet Size

Water Requirements 💧 💧💧 💧💧💧

Sunlight ☀ ☀ ⬤

- [ ] Seed
- [ ] Division
- [ ] Start
- [ ] Seed Potato
- [ ] Cutting
- [ ] Seed Garlic
- [ ] Fruit Tree/Bush
- [ ] Certified Organic
- [ ] Rooting Hormone
- [ ] Inoculant

Date	Event

Notes   [ ] Gro-Lights [ ] Thinning [ ] Potting On [ ] Hardening Off [ ] Cold Frame

Planting Medium   Damping Off Problems? [ ] Yes [ ] No

Fertilizers   [ ] Organic [ ] Liquid [ ] Time-Release

Germination Rate   [ ] Poor [ ] Average [ ] Good [ ] Excellent

Seed Company _____ Price:_____

Plant Name
Botanical Name

Date Started
Packet Size

Water
Requirements 💧 💧💧 💧💧💧   Sunlight ☀ 🌤 ⬤

☐ Seed   ☐ Start   ☐ Cutting   ☐ Fruit Tree/Bush   ☐ Rooting Hormone
☐ Division   ☐ Seed Potato ☐ Seed Garlic   ☐ Certified Organic ☐ Inoculant

Date	Event

Notes   ☐ Gro-Lights ☐ Thinning ☐ Potting On ☐ Hardening Off ☐ Cold Frame

Planting Medium   Damping Off Problems? ☐ Yes ☐ No

Fertilizers   ☐ Organic ☐ Liquid ☐ Time-Release

Germination Rate   ☐ Poor ☐ Average ☐ Good ☐ Excellent

Seed Company _____   Price:_____

Plant Name
Botanical Name

Date Started
Packet Size

Water Requirements 💧 💧💧 💧💧💧   Sunlight ☀ ◐ ●

☐ Seed ☐ Start ☐ Cutting ☐ Fruit Tree/Bush ☐ Rooting Hormone

☐ Division ☐ Seed Potato ☐ Seed Garlic ☐ Certified Organic ☐ Inoculant

Date	Event

Notes   ☐ Gro-Lights ☐ Thinning ☐ Potting On ☐ Hardening Off ☐ Cold Frame

Planting Medium   Damping Off Problems? ☐ Yes ☐ No

Fertilizers   ☐ Organic ☐ Liquid ☐ Time-Release

Germination Rate   ☐ Poor ☐ Average ☐ Good ☐ Excellent

Seed Company _____ Price:_____

Plant Name
Botanical Name

Date Started
Packet Size

Water Requirements 💧 💧💧 💧💧💧

Sunlight ☀ 🌤 ⚫

☐ Seed   ☐ Start   ☐ Cutting   ☐ Fruit Tree/Bush   ☐ Rooting Hormone
☐ Division ☐ Seed Potato ☐ Seed Garlic ☐ Certified Organic ☐ Inoculant

Date	Event

Notes   ☐ Gro-Lights ☐ Thinning ☐ Potting On ☐ Hardening Off ☐ Cold Frame

Planting Medium   Damping Off Problems? ☐ Yes ☐ No

Fertilizers   ☐ Organic ☐ Liquid ☐ Time-Release

Germination Rate   ☐ Poor ☐ Average ☐ Good ☐ Excellent

Seed Company _____   Price:_____

Plant Name	Date Started
Botanical Name	**Packet Size**

Water Requirements 💧 💧💧 💧💧💧   Sunlight ☀ ☀ ⚫

☐ Seed ☐ Start ☐ Cutting ☐ Fruit Tree/Bush ☐ Rooting Hormone

☐ Division ☐ Seed Potato ☐ Seed Garlic ☐ Certified Organic ☐ Inoculant

Date	Event

Notes   ☐ Gro-Lights ☐ Thinning ☐ Potting On ☐ Hardening Off ☐ Cold Frame

Planting Medium   Damping Off Problems? ☐ Yes ☐ No

Fertilizers   ☐ Organic ☐ Liquid ☐ Time-Release

Germination Rate   ☐ Poor ☐ Average ☐ Good ☐ Excellent

Seed Company _____   Price:_____

| **Plant Name** | **Date Started** |
| **Botanical Name** | **Packet Size** |

Water Requirements 💧 💧💧 💧💧💧   Sunlight ☀ ☼ ⬤

- ☐ Seed   ☐ Start   ☐ Cutting   ☐ Fruit Tree/Bush   ☐ Rooting Hormone
- ☐ Division ☐ Seed Potato ☐ Seed Garlic   ☐ Certified Organic   ☐ Inoculant

Date	Event

Notes   ☐ Gro-Lights ☐ Thinning ☐ Potting On ☐ Hardening Off ☐ Cold Frame

Planting Medium   Damping Off Problems? ☐ Yes ☐ No

Fertilizers   ☐ Organic   ☐ Liquid   ☐ Time-Release

Germination Rate   ☐ Poor ☐ Average ☐ Good ☐ Excellent

Seed Company _____   Price:_____

Plant Name
Botanical Name

Date Started
Packet Size

Water
Requirements 💧 💧💧 💧💧💧

Sunlight ☀ ☼ ⬤

- [ ] Seed
- [ ] Division
- [ ] Start
- [ ] Seed Potato
- [ ] Cutting
- [ ] Seed Garlic
- [ ] Fruit Tree/Bush
- [ ] Certified Organic
- [ ] Rooting Hormone
- [ ] Inoculant

Date	Event	

Notes   [ ] Gro-Lights [ ] Thinning [ ] Potting On [ ] Hardening Off [ ] Cold Frame

Planting Medium   Damping Off Problems? [ ] Yes [ ] No

Fertilizers   [ ] Organic [ ] Liquid [ ] Time-Release

Germination Rate   [ ] Poor [ ] Average [ ] Good [ ] Excellent

Seed Company _____   Price:_____

Plant Name	Date Started
Botanical Name	Packet Size

Water Requirements 🌢 🌢🌢 🌢🌢🌢   Sunlight ☀ ☀ ⬤

☐ Seed   ☐ Start   ☐ Cutting   ☐ Fruit Tree/Bush   ☐ Rooting Hormone
☐ Division   ☐ Seed Potato ☐ Seed Garlic   ☐ Certified Organic ☐ Inoculant

Date	Event

Notes   ☐ Gro-Lights ☐ Thinning ☐ Potting On ☐ Hardening Off ☐ Cold Frame

Planting Medium   Damping Off Problems? ☐ Yes ☐ No

Fertilizers   ☐ Organic ☐ Liquid ☐ Time-Release

Germination Rate   ☐ Poor ☐ Average ☐ Good ☐ Excellent

Seed Company _____ Price:_____

PLANTING

JOURNAL

SOIL PREPARATION

Plant Name
Botanical Name

Date Planted

Water
Requirements ◐ ◐◐ ◐◐◐   Sunlight ☀ ◑ ⬤

☐ Seed   ☐ Start   ☐ Cutting   ☐ Fruit Tree/Bush
☐ Division   ☐ Seed Potato   ☐ Seed Garlic   ☐ Certified Organic

Date	Event

Planting Notes & Soil Preparation   ☐ 6 Pack ☐ 4" Pot ☐ Gallon ☐ Bare Root
☐ Hardening Off ☐ Cold Frame

Fertilizers   ☐ Organic ☐ Mineral ☐ Liquid ☐ Compost ☐ Manure

Outcome & Time to Harvest

Purchased at: _____   Price: _____

Plant Name

Botanical Name

Date Planted

Water Requirements 💧 💧💧 💧💧💧   Sunlight ☀ ◑ ●

☐ Seed   ☐ Start   ☐ Cutting   ☐ Fruit Tree/Bush

☐ Division   ☐ Seed Potato   ☐ Seed Garlic   ☐ Certified Organic

Date	Event

Planting Notes & Soil Preparation   ☐ 6 Pack ☐ 4" Pot ☐ Gallon ☐ Bare Root
☐ Hardening Off ☐ Cold Frame

Fertilizers   ☐ Organic ☐ Mineral ☐ Liquid ☐ Compost ☐ Manure

Outcome & Time to Harvest

Purchased at: _____   Price: _____

Plant Name
Botanical Name

Date Planted

Water
Requirements 💧 💧💧 💧💧💧

Sunlight ☀ ◐ ●

☐ Seed ☐ Start ☐ Cutting ☐ Fruit Tree/Bush

☐ Division ☐ Seed Potato ☐ Seed Garlic ☐ Certified Organic

Date	Event

Planting Notes & Soil Preparation ☐ 6 Pack ☐ 4" Pot ☐ Gallon ☐ Bare Root
☐ Hardening Off ☐ Cold Frame

Fertilizers ☐ Organic ☐ Mineral ☐ Liquid ☐ Compost ☐ Manure

Outcome & Time to Harvest

Purchased at: _____ Price: _____

Plant Name
Botanical Name

Date Planted

Water Requirements 💧 💧💧 💧💧💧

Sunlight ☀ ◑ ⚫

☐ Seed ☐ Start ☐ Cutting ☐ Fruit Tree/Bush

☐ Division ☐ Seed Potato ☐ Seed Garlic ☐ Certified Organic

Date	Event

Planting Notes & Soil Preparation ☐ 6 Pack ☐ 4" Pot ☐ Gallon ☐ Bare Root
☐ Hardening Off ☐ Cold Frame

Fertilizers ☐ Organic ☐ Mineral ☐ Liquid ☐ Compost ☐ Manure

Outcome & Time to Harvest

Purchased at: _____ Price: _____

Plant Name	**Date Planted**
Botanical Name	

Water Requirements 💧 💧💧 💧💧💧   Sunlight ☀ ◐ ●

☐ Seed ☐ Start ☐ Cutting ☐ Fruit Tree/Bush

☐ Division ☐ Seed Potato ☐ Seed Garlic ☐ Certified Organic

Date	Event

Planting Notes & Soil Preparation ☐ 6 Pack ☐ 4" Pot ☐ Gallon ☐ Bare Root
☐ Hardening Off ☐ Cold Frame

Fertilizers ☐ Organic ☐ Mineral ☐ Liquid ☐ Compost ☐ Manure

Outcome & Time to Harvest

Purchased at: _____ Price: _____

Plant Name
Botanical Name

Date Planted

Water
Requirements 💧 💧💧 💧💧💧

Sunlight ☀ 🌓 ⚫

☐ Seed ☐ Start ☐ Cutting ☐ Fruit Tree/Bush

☐ Division ☐ Seed Potato ☐ Seed Garlic ☐ Certified Organic

Date	Event

Planting Notes & Soil Preparation ☐ 6 Pack ☐ 4" Pot ☐ Gallon ☐ Bare Root
☐ Hardening Off ☐ Cold Frame

Fertilizers ☐ Organic ☐ Mineral ☐ Liquid ☐ Compost ☐ Manure

Outcome & Time to Harvest

Purchased at: _____ Price: _____

Plant Name   **Date Planted**
Botanical Name

Water
Requirements 🌢 🌢🌢 🌢🌢🌢   Sunlight ☀ ◑ ●

☐ Seed   ☐ Start   ☐ Cutting   ☐ Fruit Tree/Bush

☐ Division   ☐ Seed Potato   ☐ Seed Garlic   ☐ Certified Organic

Date	Event

Planting Notes & Soil Preparation   ☐ 6 Pack ☐ 4" Pot ☐ Gallon ☐ Bare Root
☐ Hardening Off ☐ Cold Frame

Fertilizers   ☐ Organic ☐ Mineral ☐ Liquid ☐ Compost ☐ Manure

Outcome & Time to Harvest

Purchased at:_____   Price: _____

Plant Name　　　　　　　　　　　**Date Planted**
Botanical Name

Water
Requirements　💧　💧💧　💧💧💧　　Sunlight　☀　◑　⚫

☐ Seed　　☐ Start　　☐ Cutting　　☐ Fruit Tree/Bush

☐ Division　☐ Seed Potato　☐ Seed Garlic　☐ Certified Organic

Date	Event

Planting Notes & Soil Preparation　☐ 6 Pack　☐ 4" Pot　☐ Gallon　☐ Bare Root
☐ Hardening Off　☐ Cold Frame

Fertilizers　　　☐ Organic　☐ Mineral　☐ Liquid　☐ Compost　☐ Manure

Outcome & Time to Harvest

Purchased at: _____　Price: _____

Plant Name
Botanical Name

Date Planted

Water Requirements 💧 💧💧 💧💧💧   Sunlight ☀ ◐ ●

☐ Seed   ☐ Start   ☐ Cutting   ☐ Fruit Tree/Bush

☐ Division   ☐ Seed Potato   ☐ Seed Garlic   ☐ Certified Organic

Date	Event

Planting Notes & Soil Preparation   ☐ 6 Pack ☐ 4" Pot ☐ Gallon ☐ Bare Root
☐ Hardening Off ☐ Cold Frame

Fertilizers   ☐ Organic ☐ Mineral ☐ Liquid ☐ Compost ☐ Manure

Outcome & Time to Harvest

Purchased at: _____   Price: _____

Plant Name
Botanical Name

Date Planted

Water Requirements 💧 💧💧 💧💧💧   Sunlight ☀ ◐ ●

☐ Seed   ☐ Start   ☐ Cutting   ☐ Fruit Tree/Bush

☐ Division   ☐ Seed Potato   ☐ Seed Garlic   ☐ Certified Organic

Date	Event

Planting Notes & Soil Preparation   ☐ 6 Pack ☐ 4" Pot ☐ Gallon ☐ Bare Root
☐ Hardening Off ☐ Cold Frame

Fertilizers   ☐ Organic ☐ Mineral ☐ Liquid ☐ Compost ☐ Manure

Outcome & Time to Harvest

Purchased at:_____   Price: _____

Plant Name
Botanical Name

Date Planted

Water
Requirements 💧 💧💧 💧💧💧

Sunlight ☀ ☼ ●

☐ Seed   ☐ Start   ☐ Cutting   ☐ Fruit Tree/Bush

☐ Division   ☐ Seed Potato   ☐ Seed Garlic   ☐ Certified Organic

Date	Event

Planting Notes & Soil Preparation   ☐ 6 Pack   ☐ 4" Pot   ☐ Gallon   ☐ Bare Root
☐ Hardening Off   ☐ Cold Frame

Fertilizers   ☐ Organic   ☐ Mineral   ☐ Liquid   ☐ Compost   ☐ Manure

Outcome & Time to Harvest

Purchased at: _____   Price: _____

Plant Name
Botanical Name

Date Planted

Water Requirements 💧 💧💧 💧💧💧   Sunlight ☀ ◐ ●

☐ Seed ☐ Start ☐ Cutting ☐ Fruit Tree/Bush

☐ Division ☐ Seed Potato ☐ Seed Garlic ☐ Certified Organic

Date	Event

Planting Notes & Soil Preparation ☐ 6 Pack ☐ 4" Pot ☐ Gallon ☐ Bare Root
☐ Hardening Off ☐ Cold Frame

Fertilizers ☐ Organic ☐ Mineral ☐ Liquid ☐ Compost ☐ Manure

Outcome & Time to Harvest

Purchased at: _____ Price: _____

Plant Name
Botanical Name

Date Planted

Water
Requirements 🌢 🌢🌢 🌢🌢🌢   Sunlight ☀ ◐ ●

☐ Seed   ☐ Start   ☐ Cutting   ☐ Fruit Tree/Bush

☐ Division ☐ Seed Potato ☐ Seed Garlic ☐ Certified Organic

Date	Event

Planting Notes & Soil Preparation   ☐ 6 Pack ☐ 4" Pot ☐ Gallon ☐ Bare Root
☐ Hardening Off ☐ Cold Frame

Fertilizers   ☐ Organic ☐ Mineral ☐ Liquid ☐ Compost ☐ Manure

Outcome & Time to Harvest

Purchased at: _____ Price: _____

Plant Name
Botanical Name

Date Planted

Water
Requirements 💧 💧💧 💧💧💧

Sunlight ☀ ☼ ●

- ☐ Seed   ☐ Start   ☐ Cutting   ☐ Fruit Tree/Bush
- ☐ Division   ☐ Seed Potato   ☐ Seed Garlic   ☐ Certified Organic

Date	Event

Planting Notes & Soil Preparation   ☐ 6 Pack ☐ 4" Pot ☐ Gallon ☐ Bare Root
☐ Hardening Off ☐ Cold Frame

Fertilizers   ☐ Organic ☐ Mineral ☐ Liquid ☐ Compost ☐ Manure

Outcome & Time to Harvest

Purchased at: _____   Price: _____

Plant Name
Botanical Name

Date Planted

Water
Requirements 💧 💧💧 💧💧💧

Sunlight ☀ ◑ ●

☐ Seed ☐ Start ☐ Cutting ☐ Fruit Tree/Bush

☐ Division ☐ Seed Potato ☐ Seed Garlic ☐ Certified Organic

Date	Event

Planting Notes & Soil Preparation ☐ 6 Pack ☐ 4" Pot ☐ Gallon ☐ Bare Root
☐ Hardening Off ☐ Cold Frame

Fertilizers ☐ Organic ☐ Mineral ☐ Liquid ☐ Compost ☐ Manure

Outcome & Time to Harvest

Purchased at: _____ Price: _____

Plant Name
Botanical Name

Date Planted

Water Requirements 💧 💧💧 💧💧💧

Sunlight ☀ 🌤 ⚫

- ☐ Seed   ☐ Start   ☐ Cutting   ☐ Fruit Tree/Bush
- ☐ Division   ☐ Seed Potato   ☐ Seed Garlic   ☐ Certified Organic

Date	Event

Planting Notes & Soil Preparation   ☐ 6 Pack   ☐ 4" Pot   ☐ Gallon   ☐ Bare Root
☐ Hardening Off   ☐ Cold Frame

Fertilizers   ☐ Organic   ☐ Mineral   ☐ Liquid   ☐ Compost   ☐ Manure

Outcome & Time to Harvest

Purchased at: _____   Price: _____

Plant Name
Botanical Name

Date Planted

Water
Requirements 🌢 🌢🌢 🌢🌢🌢   Sunlight ☀ ◐ ●

☐ Seed ☐ Start ☐ Cutting ☐ Fruit Tree/Bush

☐ Division ☐ Seed Potato ☐ Seed Garlic ☐ Certified Organic

Date	Event

Planting Notes & Soil Preparation ☐ 6 Pack ☐ 4" Pot ☐ Gallon ☐ Bare Root
☐ Hardening Off ☐ Cold Frame

Fertilizers ☐ Organic ☐ Mineral ☐ Liquid ☐ Compost ☐ Manure

Outcome & Time to Harvest

Purchased at: _____ Price: _____

Plant Name
Botanical Name

Date Planted

Water
Requirements 💧 💧💧 💧💧💧

Sunlight ☀ ◑ ●

☐ Seed ☐ Start ☐ Cutting ☐ Fruit Tree/Bush

☐ Division ☐ Seed Potato ☐ Seed Garlic ☐ Certified Organic

Date	Event

Planting Notes & Soil Preparation ☐ 6 Pack ☐ 4" Pot ☐ Gallon ☐ Bare Root
☐ Hardening Off ☐ Cold Frame

Fertilizers ☐ Organic ☐ Mineral ☐ Liquid ☐ Compost ☐ Manure

Outcome & Time to Harvest

Purchased at: _____ Price: _____

Plant Name
Botanical Name

Date Planted

Water
Requirements 🌢 🌢🌢 🌢🌢🌢   Sunlight ☀ ☀ ⬤

☐ Seed ☐ Start ☐ Cutting ☐ Fruit Tree/Bush

☐ Division ☐ Seed Potato ☐ Seed Garlic ☐ Certified Organic

Date	Event

Planting Notes & Soil Preparation ☐ 6 Pack ☐ 4" Pot ☐ Gallon ☐ Bare Root
☐ Hardening Off ☐ Cold Frame

Fertilizers ☐ Organic ☐ Mineral ☐ Liquid ☐ Compost ☐ Manure

Outcome & Time to Harvest

Purchased at: _____ Price: _____

Plant Name
Botanical Name

Date Planted

Water
Requirements   💧   💧💧   💧💧💧   Sunlight   ☀   ◐   ⬤

☐ Seed   ☐ Start   ☐ Cutting   ☐ Fruit Tree/Bush

☐ Division   ☐ Seed Potato   ☐ Seed Garlic   ☐ Certified Organic

Date	Event

Planting Notes & Soil Preparation   ☐ 6 Pack   ☐ 4" Pot   ☐ Gallon   ☐ Bare Root
☐ Hardening Off   ☐ Cold Frame

Fertilizers   ☐ Organic   ☐ Mineral   ☐ Liquid   ☐ Compost   ☐ Manure

Outcome & Time to Harvest

Purchased at: _____   Price: _____

Plant Name
Botanical Name

Date Planted

Water
Requirements   💧   💧💧   💧💧💧   Sunlight   ☀   ◑   ●

☐ Seed   ☐ Start   ☐ Cutting   ☐ Fruit Tree/Bush

☐ Division ☐ Seed Potato ☐ Seed Garlic ☐ Certified Organic

Date	Event

Planting Notes & Soil Preparation   ☐ 6 Pack ☐ 4" Pot ☐ Gallon ☐ Bare Root
☐ Hardening Off ☐ Cold Frame

Fertilizers   ☐ Organic ☐ Mineral ☐ Liquid ☐ Compost ☐ Manure

Outcome & Time to Harvest

Purchased at: _____   Price: _____

Plant Name
Botanical Name

Date Planted

Water
Requirements 💧 💧💧 💧💧💧   Sunlight ☀ ◐ ●

☐ Seed ☐ Start ☐ Cutting ☐ Fruit Tree/Bush

☐ Division ☐ Seed Potato ☐ Seed Garlic ☐ Certified Organic

Date	Event

Planting Notes & Soil Preparation ☐ 6 Pack ☐ 4" Pot ☐ Gallon ☐ Bare Root
☐ Hardening Off ☐ Cold Frame

Fertilizers ☐ Organic ☐ Mineral ☐ Liquid ☐ Compost ☐ Manure

Outcome & Time to Harvest

Purchased at: _____ Price: _____

Plant Name
Botanical Name

Date Planted

Water Requirements 🌢 🌢🌢 🌢🌢🌢

Sunlight ☀ ◐ ⬤

☐ Seed ☐ Start ☐ Cutting ☐ Fruit Tree/Bush

☐ Division ☐ Seed Potato ☐ Seed Garlic ☐ Certified Organic

Date	Event

Planting Notes & Soil Preparation ☐ 6 Pack ☐ 4" Pot ☐ Gallon ☐ Bare Root
☐ Hardening Off ☐ Cold Frame

Fertilizers ☐ Organic ☐ Mineral ☐ Liquid ☐ Compost ☐ Manure

Outcome & Time to Harvest

Purchased at:_____ Price:_____

Plant Name
Botanical Name

Date Planted

Water
Requirements 💧 💧💧 💧💧💧

Sunlight ☀ ◐ ●

☐ Seed ☐ Start ☐ Cutting ☐ Fruit Tree/Bush
☐ Division ☐ Seed Potato ☐ Seed Garlic ☐ Certified Organic

Date	Event

Planting Notes & Soil Preparation   ☐ 6 Pack ☐ 4" Pot ☐ Gallon ☐ Bare Root
☐ Hardening Off ☐ Cold Frame

Fertilizers   ☐ Organic ☐ Mineral ☐ Liquid ☐ Compost ☐ Manure

Outcome & Time to Harvest

Purchased at: _____   Price: _____

Plant Name
Botanical Name

Date Planted

Water Requirements 💧 💧💧 💧💧💧   Sunlight ☀ ◐ ●

☐ Seed ☐ Start ☐ Cutting ☐ Fruit Tree/Bush

☐ Division ☐ Seed Potato ☐ Seed Garlic ☐ Certified Organic

Date	Event

Planting Notes & Soil Preparation ☐ 6 Pack ☐ 4" Pot ☐ Gallon ☐ Bare Root
☐ Hardening Off ☐ Cold Frame

Fertilizers ☐ Organic ☐ Mineral ☐ Liquid ☐ Compost ☐ Manure

Outcome & Time to Harvest

Purchased at: _____   Price: _____

Plant Name
Botanical Name

Date Planted

Water
Requirements   💧   💧💧   💧💧💧

Sunlight   ☀   ◐   ⚫

☐ Seed   ☐ Start   ☐ Cutting   ☐ Fruit Tree/Bush

☐ Division   ☐ Seed Potato   ☐ Seed Garlic   ☐ Certified Organic

Date	Event

Planting Notes & Soil Preparation   ☐ 6 Pack ☐ 4" Pot ☐ Gallon ☐ Bare Root
☐ Hardening Off ☐ Cold Frame

Fertilizers   ☐ Organic ☐ Mineral ☐ Liquid ☐ Compost ☐ Manure

Outcome & Time to Harvest

Purchased at: _____   Price: _____

Plant Name
Botanical Name

Date Planted

Water
Requirements
💧 💧💧 💧💧💧

Sunlight ☀ ☀ ⚫

☐ Seed ☐ Start ☐ Cutting ☐ Fruit Tree/Bush

☐ Division ☐ Seed Potato ☐ Seed Garlic ☐ Certified Organic

Date	Event

Planting Notes & Soil Preparation ☐ 6 Pack ☐ 4" Pot ☐ Gallon ☐ Bare Root
☐ Hardening Off ☐ Cold Frame

Fertilizers ☐ Organic ☐ Mineral ☐ Liquid ☐ Compost ☐ Manure

Outcome & Time to Harvest

Purchased at: _____ Price: _____

Plant Name
Botanical Name

Date Planted

Water
Requirements   💧   💧💧   💧💧💧   Sunlight   ☀   ◐   ●

☐ Seed   ☐ Start   ☐ Cutting   ☐ Fruit Tree/Bush
☐ Division ☐ Seed Potato ☐ Seed Garlic ☐ Certified Organic

Date	Event

Planting Notes & Soil Preparation   ☐ 6 Pack ☐ 4" Pot ☐ Gallon ☐ Bare Root
☐ Hardening Off ☐ Cold Frame

Fertilizers   ☐ Organic ☐ Mineral ☐ Liquid ☐ Compost ☐ Manure

Outcome & Time to Harvest

Purchased at: _____   Price: _____

Plant Name
Botanical Name

Date Planted

Water
Requirements   💧   💧💧   💧💧💧   Sunlight   ☀   🌓   ⚫

☐ Seed   ☐ Start   ☐ Cutting   ☐ Fruit Tree/Bush

☐ Division   ☐ Seed Potato   ☐ Seed Garlic   ☐ Certified Organic

Date	Event

Planting Notes & Soil Preparation   ☐ 6 Pack   ☐ 4" Pot   ☐ Gallon   ☐ Bare Root
☐ Hardening Off   ☐ Cold Frame

Fertilizers   ☐ Organic   ☐ Mineral   ☐ Liquid   ☐ Compost   ☐ Manure

Outcome & Time to Harvest

Purchased at: _____   Price: _____

Plant Name
Botanical Name

Date Planted

Water
Requirements 💧 💧💧 💧💧💧

Sunlight ☀ ◑ ●

☐ Seed ☐ Start ☐ Cutting ☐ Fruit Tree/Bush
☐ Division ☐ Seed Potato ☐ Seed Garlic ☐ Certified Organic

Date	Event

Planting Notes & Soil Preparation ☐ 6 Pack ☐ 4" Pot ☐ Gallon ☐ Bare Root
☐ Hardening Off ☐ Cold Frame

Fertilizers ☐ Organic ☐ Mineral ☐ Liquid ☐ Compost ☐ Manure

Outcome & Time to Harvest

Purchased at: _____ Price: _____

Plant Name
Botanical Name

Date Planted

Water
Requirements 💧 💧💧 💧💧💧

Sunlight ☀ ◐ ●

- ☐ Seed ☐ Start ☐ Cutting ☐ Fruit Tree/Bush
- ☐ Division ☐ Seed Potato ☐ Seed Garlic ☐ Certified Organic

Date	Event

Planting Notes & Soil Preparation ☐ 6 Pack ☐ 4" Pot ☐ Gallon ☐ Bare Root
☐ Hardening Off ☐ Cold Frame

Fertilizers ☐ Organic ☐ Mineral ☐ Liquid ☐ Compost ☐ Manure

Outcome & Time to Harvest

Purchased at: _____ Price: _____

Date _____

Type of Plants _____

Waxing			Full Moon		Waning	

Plants

Fertilizers

Weather and Temperature
Cloches & Cold Frames

Follow Up

Results _____

_____

PLANTING BY THE MOON

Date _____

Type of Plants _____

Waxing			Full Moon		Waning	

Plants

_____
_____
_____
_____
_____

Fertilizers

_____
_____
_____
_____
_____
_____
_____
_____
_____
_____
_____

Weather and Temperature
Cloches & Cold Frames

_____
_____
_____
_____
_____

Follow Up

Results _____

_____

NOTES
&
OBSERVATIONS

JOURNAL

FERTILIZER NOTES

☐ Organic ☐ Chemical ☐ Time Release ☐ Liquid
☐ Mineral ☐ Animal ☐ Compost ☐ Manure

BRAND NAME	SOURCE	N-P-K	DATE APPLIED	ISSUES?

FERTILIZER NOTES

☐ Organic ☐ Chemical ☐ Time Release ☐ Liquid
☐ Mineral ☐ Animal ☐ Compost ☐ Manure

BRAND NAME	SOURCE	N-P-K	DATE APPLIED	ISSUES?

FERTILIZER NOTES

☐ Organic ☐ Chemical ☐ Time Release ☐ Liquid
☐ Mineral ☐ Animal ☐ Compost ☐ Manure

BRAND NAME	SOURCE	N-P-K	DATE APPLIED	ISSUES?

FERTILIZER NOTES

- [ ] Organic [ ] Chemical [ ] Time Release [ ] Liquid
- [ ] Mineral [ ] Animal [ ] Compost [ ] Manure

BRAND NAME	SOURCE	N-P-K	DATE APPLIED	ISSUES?

FERTILIZER NOTES

☐ Organic ☐ Chemical ☐ Time Release ☐ Liquid
☐ Mineral ☐ Animal ☐ Compost ☐ Manure

BRAND NAME	SOURCE	N-P-K	DATE APPLIED	ISSUES?

FERTILIZER NOTES

☐ Organic ☐ Chemical ☐ Time Release ☐ Liquid
☐ Mineral ☐ Animal ☐ Compost ☐ Manure

BRAND NAME	SOURCE	N-P-K	DATE APPLIED	ISSUES?

FERTILIZER NOTES

- [ ] Organic [ ] Chemical [ ] Time Release [ ] Liquid
- [ ] Mineral [ ] Animal [ ] Compost [ ] Manure

BRAND NAME	SOURCE	N-P-K	DATE APPLIED	ISSUES?

GARDENING UNDER COVER

● Cold Frame ● Row Cover
● Greenhouse ● Porch/Garage etc

PLANT	DATES	TYPE OF PROTECTION

GARDENING UNDER COVER

● Cold Frame   ● Row Cover
● Greenhouse   ● Porch/Garage etc

PLANT	DATES	TYPE OF PROTECTION

GARDENING UNDER COVER

● Cold Frame   ● Row Cover
● Greenhouse   ● Porch/Garage etc

PLANT	DATES	TYPE OF PROTECTION

GARDENING UNDER COVER

● Cold Frame   ● Row Cover
● Greenhouse   ● Porch/Garage etc

PLANT	DATES	TYPE OF PROTECTION

GARDENING UNDER COVER

● Cold Frame   ● Row Cover
● Greenhouse   ● Porch/Garage etc

PLANT	DATES	TYPE OF PROTECTION

PEST CONTROL NOTES

☐ Natural ☐ Chemical ☐ Broad Spectrum
☐ Pelleted ☐ Liquid ☐ Beneficial Insects

BRAND NAME	TARGET PEST	DATE APPLIED	ISSUES?

PEST CONTROL NOTES

☐ Natural ☐ Chemical ☐ Broad Spectrum
☐ Pelleted ☐ Liquid ☐ Beneficial Insects

BRAND NAME	TARGET PEST	DATE APPLIED	ISSUES?

PEST CONTROL NOTES

☐ Natural ☐ Chemical ☐ Broad Spectrum
☐ Pelleted ☐ Liquid ☐ Beneficial Insects

BRAND NAME	TARGET PEST	DATE APPLIED	ISSUES?

PEST CONTROL NOTES

- [ ] Natural [ ] Chemical [ ] Broad Spectrum
- [ ] Pelleted [ ] Liquid [ ] Beneficial Insects

BRAND NAME	TARGET PEST	DATE APPLIED	ISSUES?

PEST CONTROL NOTES

☐ Natural   ☐ Chemical   ☐ Broad Spectrum
☐ Pelleted   ☐ Liquid   ☐ Beneficial Insects

BRAND NAME	TARGET PEST	DATE APPLIED	ISSUES?

PEST CONTROL NOTES

☐ Natural ☐ Chemical ☐ Broad Spectrum
☐ Pelleted ☐ Liquid ☐ Beneficial Insects

BRAND NAME	TARGET PEST	DATE APPLIED	ISSUES?

PEST CONTROL NOTES

☐ Natural ☐ Chemical ☐ Broad Spectrum
☐ Pelleted ☐ Liquid ☐ Beneficial Insects

BRAND NAME	TARGET PEST	DATE APPLIED	ISSUES?

HARVEST NOTES

☐ Vegetable ☐ Fruit ☐ Root
☐ Vine ☐ Tree ☐ Bush

PLANT	YIELD	YOUR RATING						
		My Rating This Year	○	○	○	○	○
		Previous Years	○	○	○	○	○
		My Rating This Year	○	○	○	○	○
		Previous Years	○	○	○	○	○
		My Rating This Year	○	○	○	○	○
		Previous Years	○	○	○	○	○
		My Rating This Year	○	○	○	○	○
		Previous Years	○	○	○	○	○
		My Rating This Year	○	○	○	○	○
		Previous Years	○	○	○	○	○
		My Rating This Year	○	○	○	○	○
		Previous Years	○	○	○	○	○
		My Rating This Year	○	○	○	○	○
		Previous Years	○	○	○	○	○
		My Rating This Year	○	○	○	○	○
		Previous Years	○	○	○	○	○
		My Rating This Year	○	○	○	○	○
		Previous Years	○	○	○	○	○
		My Rating This Year	○	○	○	○	○
		Previous Years	○	○	○	○	○
		My Rating This Year	○	○	○	○	○
		Previous Years	○	○	○	○	○
		My Rating This Year	○	○	○	○	○
		Previous Years	○	○	○	○	○
		My Rating This Year	○	○	○	○	○
		Previous Years	○	○	○	○	○
		My Rating This Year	○	○	○	○	○
		Previous Years	○	○	○	○	○
		My Rating This Year	○	○	○	○	○
		Previous Years	○	○	○	○	○
		My Rating This Year	○	○	○	○	○
		Previous Years	○	○	○	○	○
		My Rating This Year	○	○	○	○	○
		Previous Years	○	○	○	○	○
		My Rating This Year	○	○	○	○	○
		Previous Years	○	○	○	○	○
		My Rating This Year	○	○	○	○	○
		Previous Years	○	○	○	○	○
		My Rating This Year	○	○	○	○	○
		Previous Years	○	○	○	○	○
		My Rating This Year	○	○	○	○	○
		Previous Years	○	○	○	○	○
		My Rating This Year	○	○	○	○	○
		Previous Years	○	○	○	○	○

HARVEST NOTES

☐ Vegetable ☐ Fruit ☐ Root
☐ Vine ☐ Tree ☐ Bush

PLANT	YIELD	YOUR RATING	
		My Rating This Year	○ ○ ○ ○ ○
		Previous Years	○ ○ ○ ○ ○
		My Rating This Year	○ ○ ○ ○ ○
		Previous Years	○ ○ ○ ○ ○
		My Rating This Year	○ ○ ○ ○ ○
		Previous Years	○ ○ ○ ○ ○
		My Rating This Year	○ ○ ○ ○ ○
		Previous Years	○ ○ ○ ○ ○
		My Rating This Year	○ ○ ○ ○ ○
		Previous Years	○ ○ ○ ○ ○
		My Rating This Year	○ ○ ○ ○ ○
		Previous Years	○ ○ ○ ○ ○
		My Rating This Year	○ ○ ○ ○ ○
		Previous Years	○ ○ ○ ○ ○
		My Rating This Year	○ ○ ○ ○ ○
		Previous Years	○ ○ ○ ○ ○
		My Rating This Year	○ ○ ○ ○ ○
		Previous Years	○ ○ ○ ○ ○
		My Rating This Year	○ ○ ○ ○ ○
		Previous Years	○ ○ ○ ○ ○
		My Rating This Year	○ ○ ○ ○ ○
		Previous Years	○ ○ ○ ○ ○
		My Rating This Year	○ ○ ○ ○ ○
		Previous Years	○ ○ ○ ○ ○
		My Rating This Year	○ ○ ○ ○ ○
		Previous Years	○ ○ ○ ○ ○
		My Rating This Year	○ ○ ○ ○ ○
		Previous Years	○ ○ ○ ○ ○
		My Rating This Year	○ ○ ○ ○ ○
		Previous Years	○ ○ ○ ○ ○
		My Rating This Year	○ ○ ○ ○ ○
		Previous Years	○ ○ ○ ○ ○
		My Rating This Year	○ ○ ○ ○ ○
		Previous Years	○ ○ ○ ○ ○
		My Rating This Year	○ ○ ○ ○ ○
		Previous Years	○ ○ ○ ○ ○
		My Rating This Year	○ ○ ○ ○ ○
		Previous Years	○ ○ ○ ○ ○
		My Rating This Year	○ ○ ○ ○ ○
		Previous Years	○ ○ ○ ○ ○
		My Rating This Year	○ ○ ○ ○ ○
		Previous Years	○ ○ ○ ○ ○
		My Rating This Year	○ ○ ○ ○ ○
		Previous Years	○ ○ ○ ○ ○

HARVEST NOTES

☐ Vegetable ☐ Fruit ☐ Root
☐ Vine ☐ Tree ☐ Bush

PLANT	YIELD	YOUR RATING					
		My Rating This Year	○	○	○	○	○
		Previous Years	○	○	○	○	○
		My Rating This Year	○	○	○	○	○
		Previous Years	○	○	○	○	○
		My Rating This Year	○	○	○	○	○
		Previous Years	○	○	○	○	○
		My Rating This Year	○	○	○	○	○
		Previous Years	○	○	○	○	○
		My Rating This Year	○	○	○	○	○
		Previous Years	○	○	○	○	○
		My Rating This Year	○	○	○	○	○
		Previous Years	○	○	○	○	○
		My Rating This Year	○	○	○	○	○
		Previous Years	○	○	○	○	○
		My Rating This Year	○	○	○	○	○
		Previous Years	○	○	○	○	○
		My Rating This Year	○	○	○	○	○
		Previous Years	○	○	○	○	○
		My Rating This Year	○	○	○	○	○
		Previous Years	○	○	○	○	○
		My Rating This Year	○	○	○	○	○
		Previous Years	○	○	○	○	○
		My Rating This Year	○	○	○	○	○
		Previous Years	○	○	○	○	○
		My Rating This Year	○	○	○	○	○
		Previous Years	○	○	○	○	○
		My Rating This Year	○	○	○	○	○
		Previous Years	○	○	○	○	○
		My Rating This Year	○	○	○	○	○
		Previous Years	○	○	○	○	○
		My Rating This Year	○	○	○	○	○
		Previous Years	○	○	○	○	○
		My Rating This Year	○	○	○	○	○
		Previous Years	○	○	○	○	○
		My Rating This Year	○	○	○	○	○
		Previous Years	○	○	○	○	○
		My Rating This Year	○	○	○	○	○
		Previous Years	○	○	○	○	○
		My Rating This Year	○	○	○	○	○
		Previous Years	○	○	○	○	○
		My Rating This Year	○	○	○	○	○
		Previous Years	○	○	○	○	○

HARVEST NOTES

☐ Vegetable ☐ Fruit ☐ Root
☐ Vine ☐ Tree ☐ Bush

PLANT	YIELD	YOUR RATING	
		My Rating This Year	○ ○ ○ ○ ○
		Previous Years	○ ○ ○ ○ ○
		My Rating This Year	○ ○ ○ ○ ○
		Previous Years	○ ○ ○ ○ ○
		My Rating This Year	○ ○ ○ ○ ○
		Previous Years	○ ○ ○ ○ ○
		My Rating This Year	○ ○ ○ ○ ○
		Previous Years	○ ○ ○ ○ ○
		My Rating This Year	○ ○ ○ ○ ○
		Previous Years	○ ○ ○ ○ ○
		My Rating This Year	○ ○ ○ ○ ○
		Previous Years	○ ○ ○ ○ ○
		My Rating This Year	○ ○ ○ ○ ○
		Previous Years	○ ○ ○ ○ ○
		My Rating This Year	○ ○ ○ ○ ○
		Previous Years	○ ○ ○ ○ ○
		My Rating This Year	○ ○ ○ ○ ○
		Previous Years	○ ○ ○ ○ ○
		My Rating This Year	○ ○ ○ ○ ○
		Previous Years	○ ○ ○ ○ ○
		My Rating This Year	○ ○ ○ ○ ○
		Previous Years	○ ○ ○ ○ ○
		My Rating This Year	○ ○ ○ ○ ○
		Previous Years	○ ○ ○ ○ ○
		My Rating This Year	○ ○ ○ ○ ○
		Previous Years	○ ○ ○ ○ ○
		My Rating This Year	○ ○ ○ ○ ○
		Previous Years	○ ○ ○ ○ ○
		My Rating This Year	○ ○ ○ ○ ○
		Previous Years	○ ○ ○ ○ ○
		My Rating This Year	○ ○ ○ ○ ○
		Previous Years	○ ○ ○ ○ ○
		My Rating This Year	○ ○ ○ ○ ○
		Previous Years	○ ○ ○ ○ ○
		My Rating This Year	○ ○ ○ ○ ○
		Previous Years	○ ○ ○ ○ ○
		My Rating This Year	○ ○ ○ ○ ○
		Previous Years	○ ○ ○ ○ ○
		My Rating This Year	○ ○ ○ ○ ○
		Previous Years	○ ○ ○ ○ ○
		My Rating This Year	○ ○ ○ ○ ○
		Previous Years	○ ○ ○ ○ ○
		My Rating This Year	○ ○ ○ ○ ○
		Previous Years	○ ○ ○ ○ ○

HARVEST NOTES

☐ Vegetable ☐ Fruit ☐ Root
☐ Vine   ☐ Tree   ☐ Bush

PLANT	YIELD	YOUR RATING	
		My Rating This Year	○ ○ ○ ○ ○
		Previous Years	○ ○ ○ ○ ○
		My Rating This Year	○ ○ ○ ○ ○
		Previous Years	○ ○ ○ ○ ○
		My Rating This Year	○ ○ ○ ○ ○
		Previous Years	○ ○ ○ ○ ○
		My Rating This Year	○ ○ ○ ○ ○
		Previous Years	○ ○ ○ ○ ○
		My Rating This Year	○ ○ ○ ○ ○
		Previous Years	○ ○ ○ ○ ○
		My Rating This Year	○ ○ ○ ○ ○
		Previous Years	○ ○ ○ ○ ○
		My Rating This Year	○ ○ ○ ○ ○
		Previous Years	○ ○ ○ ○ ○
		My Rating This Year	○ ○ ○ ○ ○
		Previous Years	○ ○ ○ ○ ○
		My Rating This Year	○ ○ ○ ○ ○
		Previous Years	○ ○ ○ ○ ○
		My Rating This Year	○ ○ ○ ○ ○
		Previous Years	○ ○ ○ ○ ○
		My Rating This Year	○ ○ ○ ○ ○
		Previous Years	○ ○ ○ ○ ○
		My Rating This Year	○ ○ ○ ○ ○
		Previous Years	○ ○ ○ ○ ○
		My Rating This Year	○ ○ ○ ○ ○
		Previous Years	○ ○ ○ ○ ○
		My Rating This Year	○ ○ ○ ○ ○
		Previous Years	○ ○ ○ ○ ○
		My Rating This Year	○ ○ ○ ○ ○
		Previous Years	○ ○ ○ ○ ○
		My Rating This Year	○ ○ ○ ○ ○
		Previous Years	○ ○ ○ ○ ○
		My Rating This Year	○ ○ ○ ○ ○
		Previous Years	○ ○ ○ ○ ○
		My Rating This Year	○ ○ ○ ○ ○
		Previous Years	○ ○ ○ ○ ○
		My Rating This Year	○ ○ ○ ○ ○
		Previous Years	○ ○ ○ ○ ○
		My Rating This Year	○ ○ ○ ○ ○
		Previous Years	○ ○ ○ ○ ○
		My Rating This Year	○ ○ ○ ○ ○
		Previous Years	○ ○ ○ ○ ○
		My Rating This Year	○ ○ ○ ○ ○
		Previous Years	○ ○ ○ ○ ○

HARVEST NOTES

PLANT	YIELD	YOUR RATING						
		My Rating This Year	○	○	○	○	○	
		Previous Years	○	○	○	○	○	
		My Rating This Year	○	○	○	○	○	
		Previous Years	○	○	○	○	○	
		My Rating This Year	○	○	○	○	○	
		Previous Years	○	○	○	○	○	
		My Rating This Year	○	○	○	○	○	
		Previous Years	○	○	○	○	○	
		My Rating This Year	○	○	○	○	○	
		Previous Years	○	○	○	○	○	
		My Rating This Year	○	○	○	○	○	
		Previous Years	○	○	○	○	○	
		My Rating This Year	○	○	○	○	○	
		Previous Years	○	○	○	○	○	
		My Rating This Year	○	○	○	○	○	
		Previous Years	○	○	○	○	○	
		My Rating This Year	○	○	○	○	○	
		Previous Years	○	○	○	○	○	
		My Rating This Year	○	○	○	○	○	
		Previous Years	○	○	○	○	○	
		My Rating This Year	○	○	○	○	○	
		Previous Years	○	○	○	○	○	
		My Rating This Year	○	○	○	○	○	
		Previous Years	○	○	○	○	○	
		My Rating This Year	○	○	○	○	○	
		Previous Years	○	○	○	○	○	
		My Rating This Year	○	○	○	○	○	
		Previous Years	○	○	○	○	○	
		My Rating This Year	○	○	○	○	○	
		Previous Years	○	○	○	○	○	
		My Rating This Year	○	○	○	○	○	
		Previous Years	○	○	○	○	○	
		My Rating This Year	○	○	○	○	○	
		Previous Years	○	○	○	○	○	
		My Rating This Year	○	○	○	○	○	
		Previous Years	○	○	○	○	○	
		My Rating This Year	○	○	○	○	○	
		Previous Years	○	○	○	○	○	
		My Rating This Year	○	○	○	○	○	
		Previous Years	○	○	○	○	○	
		My Rating This Year	○	○	○	○	○	
		Previous Years	○	○	○	○	○	
		My Rating This Year	○	○	○	○	○	
		Previous Years	○	○	○	○	○	

HARVEST NOTES

☐ Vegetable ☐ Fruit ☐ Root
☐ Vine ☐ Tree ☐ Bush

PLANT	YIELD	YOUR RATING	
		My Rating This Year	○ ○ ○ ○ ○
		Previous Years	○ ○ ○ ○ ○
		My Rating This Year	○ ○ ○ ○ ○
		Previous Years	○ ○ ○ ○ ○
		My Rating This Year	○ ○ ○ ○ ○
		Previous Years	○ ○ ○ ○ ○
		My Rating This Year	○ ○ ○ ○ ○
		Previous Years	○ ○ ○ ○ ○
		My Rating This Year	○ ○ ○ ○ ○
		Previous Years	○ ○ ○ ○ ○
		My Rating This Year	○ ○ ○ ○ ○
		Previous Years	○ ○ ○ ○ ○
		My Rating This Year	○ ○ ○ ○ ○
		Previous Years	○ ○ ○ ○ ○
		My Rating This Year	○ ○ ○ ○ ○
		Previous Years	○ ○ ○ ○ ○
		My Rating This Year	○ ○ ○ ○ ○
		Previous Years	○ ○ ○ ○ ○
		My Rating This Year	○ ○ ○ ○ ○
		Previous Years	○ ○ ○ ○ ○
		My Rating This Year	○ ○ ○ ○ ○
		Previous Years	○ ○ ○ ○ ○
		My Rating This Year	○ ○ ○ ○ ○
		Previous Years	○ ○ ○ ○ ○
		My Rating This Year	○ ○ ○ ○ ○
		Previous Years	○ ○ ○ ○ ○
		My Rating This Year	○ ○ ○ ○ ○
		Previous Years	○ ○ ○ ○ ○
		My Rating This Year	○ ○ ○ ○ ○
		Previous Years	○ ○ ○ ○ ○
		My Rating This Year	○ ○ ○ ○ ○
		Previous Years	○ ○ ○ ○ ○
		My Rating This Year	○ ○ ○ ○ ○
		Previous Years	○ ○ ○ ○ ○
		My Rating This Year	○ ○ ○ ○ ○
		Previous Years	○ ○ ○ ○ ○
		My Rating This Year	○ ○ ○ ○ ○
		Previous Years	○ ○ ○ ○ ○
		My Rating This Year	○ ○ ○ ○ ○
		Previous Years	○ ○ ○ ○ ○
		My Rating This Year	○ ○ ○ ○ ○
		Previous Years	○ ○ ○ ○ ○
		My Rating This Year	○ ○ ○ ○ ○
		Previous Years	○ ○ ○ ○ ○
		My Rating This Year	○ ○ ○ ○ ○
		Previous Years	○ ○ ○ ○ ○

HARVEST NOTES

☐ Vegetable ☐ Fruit ☐ Root
☐ Vine ☐ Tree ☐ Bush

PLANT	YIELD	YOUR RATING	
		My Rating This Year	○ ○ ○ ○ ○
		Previous Years	○ ○ ○ ○ ○
		My Rating This Year	○ ○ ○ ○ ○
		Previous Years	○ ○ ○ ○ ○
		My Rating This Year	○ ○ ○ ○ ○
		Previous Years	○ ○ ○ ○ ○
		My Rating This Year	○ ○ ○ ○ ○
		Previous Years	○ ○ ○ ○ ○
		My Rating This Year	○ ○ ○ ○ ○
		Previous Years	○ ○ ○ ○ ○
		My Rating This Year	○ ○ ○ ○ ○
		Previous Years	○ ○ ○ ○ ○
		My Rating This Year	○ ○ ○ ○ ○
		Previous Years	○ ○ ○ ○ ○
		My Rating This Year	○ ○ ○ ○ ○
		Previous Years	○ ○ ○ ○ ○
		My Rating This Year	○ ○ ○ ○ ○
		Previous Years	○ ○ ○ ○ ○
		My Rating This Year	○ ○ ○ ○ ○
		Previous Years	○ ○ ○ ○ ○
		My Rating This Year	○ ○ ○ ○ ○
		Previous Years	○ ○ ○ ○ ○
		My Rating This Year	○ ○ ○ ○ ○
		Previous Years	○ ○ ○ ○ ○
		My Rating This Year	○ ○ ○ ○ ○
		Previous Years	○ ○ ○ ○ ○
		My Rating This Year	○ ○ ○ ○ ○
		Previous Years	○ ○ ○ ○ ○
		My Rating This Year	○ ○ ○ ○ ○
		Previous Years	○ ○ ○ ○ ○
		My Rating This Year	○ ○ ○ ○ ○
		Previous Years	○ ○ ○ ○ ○
		My Rating This Year	○ ○ ○ ○ ○
		Previous Years	○ ○ ○ ○ ○
		My Rating This Year	○ ○ ○ ○ ○
		Previous Years	○ ○ ○ ○ ○
		My Rating This Year	○ ○ ○ ○ ○
		Previous Years	○ ○ ○ ○ ○
		My Rating This Year	○ ○ ○ ○ ○
		Previous Years	○ ○ ○ ○ ○
		My Rating This Year	○ ○ ○ ○ ○
		Previous Years	○ ○ ○ ○ ○
		My Rating This Year	○ ○ ○ ○ ○
		Previous Years	○ ○ ○ ○ ○

HARVEST NOTES

☐ Vegetable ☐ Fruit ☐ Root
☐ Vine ☐ Tree ☐ Bush

PLANT	YIELD	YOUR RATING		
		My Rating This Year	○ ○ ○ ○ ○	
		Previous Years	○ ○ ○ ○ ○	
		My Rating This Year	○ ○ ○ ○ ○	
		Previous Years	○ ○ ○ ○ ○	
		My Rating This Year	○ ○ ○ ○ ○	
		Previous Years	○ ○ ○ ○ ○	
		My Rating This Year	○ ○ ○ ○ ○	
		Previous Years	○ ○ ○ ○ ○	
		My Rating This Year	○ ○ ○ ○ ○	
		Previous Years	○ ○ ○ ○ ○	
		My Rating This Year	○ ○ ○ ○ ○	
		Previous Years	○ ○ ○ ○ ○	
		My Rating This Year	○ ○ ○ ○ ○	
		Previous Years	○ ○ ○ ○ ○	
		My Rating This Year	○ ○ ○ ○ ○	
		Previous Years	○ ○ ○ ○ ○	
		My Rating This Year	○ ○ ○ ○ ○	
		Previous Years	○ ○ ○ ○ ○	
		My Rating This Year	○ ○ ○ ○ ○	
		Previous Years	○ ○ ○ ○ ○	
		My Rating This Year	○ ○ ○ ○ ○	
		Previous Years	○ ○ ○ ○ ○	
		My Rating This Year	○ ○ ○ ○ ○	
		Previous Years	○ ○ ○ ○ ○	
		My Rating This Year	○ ○ ○ ○ ○	
		Previous Years	○ ○ ○ ○ ○	
		My Rating This Year	○ ○ ○ ○ ○	
		Previous Years	○ ○ ○ ○ ○	
		My Rating This Year	○ ○ ○ ○ ○	
		Previous Years	○ ○ ○ ○ ○	
		My Rating This Year	○ ○ ○ ○ ○	
		Previous Years	○ ○ ○ ○ ○	
		My Rating This Year	○ ○ ○ ○ ○	
		Previous Years	○ ○ ○ ○ ○	
		My Rating This Year	○ ○ ○ ○ ○	
		Previous Years	○ ○ ○ ○ ○	
		My Rating This Year	○ ○ ○ ○ ○	
		Previous Years	○ ○ ○ ○ ○	
		My Rating This Year	○ ○ ○ ○ ○	
		Previous Years	○ ○ ○ ○ ○	
		My Rating This Year	○ ○ ○ ○ ○	
		Previous Years	○ ○ ○ ○ ○	
		My Rating This Year	○ ○ ○ ○ ○	
		Previous Years	○ ○ ○ ○ ○	
		My Rating This Year	○ ○ ○ ○ ○	
		Previous Years	○ ○ ○ ○ ○	

HARVEST NOTES

☐ Vegetable ☐ Fruit ☐ Root
☐ Vine   ☐ Tree   ☐ Bush

PLANT	YIELD	YOUR RATING	
		My Rating This Year	○ ○ ○ ○ ○
		Previous Years	○ ○ ○ ○ ○
		My Rating This Year	○ ○ ○ ○ ○
		Previous Years	○ ○ ○ ○ ○
		My Rating This Year	○ ○ ○ ○ ○
		Previous Years	○ ○ ○ ○ ○
		My Rating This Year	○ ○ ○ ○ ○
		Previous Years	○ ○ ○ ○ ○
		My Rating This Year	○ ○ ○ ○ ○
		Previous Years	○ ○ ○ ○ ○
		My Rating This Year	○ ○ ○ ○ ○
		Previous Years	○ ○ ○ ○ ○
		My Rating This Year	○ ○ ○ ○ ○
		Previous Years	○ ○ ○ ○ ○
		My Rating This Year	○ ○ ○ ○ ○
		Previous Years	○ ○ ○ ○ ○
		My Rating This Year	○ ○ ○ ○ ○
		Previous Years	○ ○ ○ ○ ○
		My Rating This Year	○ ○ ○ ○ ○
		Previous Years	○ ○ ○ ○ ○
		My Rating This Year	○ ○ ○ ○ ○
		Previous Years	○ ○ ○ ○ ○
		My Rating This Year	○ ○ ○ ○ ○
		Previous Years	○ ○ ○ ○ ○
		My Rating This Year	○ ○ ○ ○ ○
		Previous Years	○ ○ ○ ○ ○
		My Rating This Year	○ ○ ○ ○ ○
		Previous Years	○ ○ ○ ○ ○
		My Rating This Year	○ ○ ○ ○ ○
		Previous Years	○ ○ ○ ○ ○
		My Rating This Year	○ ○ ○ ○ ○
		Previous Years	○ ○ ○ ○ ○
		My Rating This Year	○ ○ ○ ○ ○
		Previous Years	○ ○ ○ ○ ○
		My Rating This Year	○ ○ ○ ○ ○
		Previous Years	○ ○ ○ ○ ○
		My Rating This Year	○ ○ ○ ○ ○
		Previous Years	○ ○ ○ ○ ○
		My Rating This Year	○ ○ ○ ○ ○
		Previous Years	○ ○ ○ ○ ○
		My Rating This Year	○ ○ ○ ○ ○
		Previous Years	○ ○ ○ ○ ○
		My Rating This Year	○ ○ ○ ○ ○
		Previous Years	○ ○ ○ ○ ○

HARVEST NOTES

☐ Vegetable ☐ Fruit ☐ Root
☐ Vine ☐ Tree ☐ Bush

PLANT	YIELD	YOUR RATING		
		My Rating This Year	○ ○ ○ ○ ○	
		Previous Years	○ ○ ○ ○ ○	
		My Rating This Year	○ ○ ○ ○ ○	
		Previous Years	○ ○ ○ ○ ○	
		My Rating This Year	○ ○ ○ ○ ○	
		Previous Years	○ ○ ○ ○ ○	
		My Rating This Year	○ ○ ○ ○ ○	
		Previous Years	○ ○ ○ ○ ○	
		My Rating This Year	○ ○ ○ ○ ○	
		Previous Years	○ ○ ○ ○ ○	
		My Rating This Year	○ ○ ○ ○ ○	
		Previous Years	○ ○ ○ ○ ○	
		My Rating This Year	○ ○ ○ ○ ○	
		Previous Years	○ ○ ○ ○ ○	
		My Rating This Year	○ ○ ○ ○ ○	
		Previous Years	○ ○ ○ ○ ○	
		My Rating This Year	○ ○ ○ ○ ○	
		Previous Years	○ ○ ○ ○ ○	
		My Rating This Year	○ ○ ○ ○ ○	
		Previous Years	○ ○ ○ ○ ○	
		My Rating This Year	○ ○ ○ ○ ○	
		Previous Years	○ ○ ○ ○ ○	
		My Rating This Year	○ ○ ○ ○ ○	
		Previous Years	○ ○ ○ ○ ○	
		My Rating This Year	○ ○ ○ ○ ○	
		Previous Years	○ ○ ○ ○ ○	
		My Rating This Year	○ ○ ○ ○ ○	
		Previous Years	○ ○ ○ ○ ○	
		My Rating This Year	○ ○ ○ ○ ○	
		Previous Years	○ ○ ○ ○ ○	
		My Rating This Year	○ ○ ○ ○ ○	
		Previous Years	○ ○ ○ ○ ○	
		My Rating This Year	○ ○ ○ ○ ○	
		Previous Years	○ ○ ○ ○ ○	
		My Rating This Year	○ ○ ○ ○ ○	
		Previous Years	○ ○ ○ ○ ○	
		My Rating This Year	○ ○ ○ ○ ○	
		Previous Years	○ ○ ○ ○ ○	
		My Rating This Year	○ ○ ○ ○ ○	
		Previous Years	○ ○ ○ ○ ○	
		My Rating This Year	○ ○ ○ ○ ○	
		Previous Years	○ ○ ○ ○ ○	
		My Rating This Year	○ ○ ○ ○ ○	
		Previous Years	○ ○ ○ ○ ○	
		My Rating This Year	○ ○ ○ ○ ○	
		Previous Years	○ ○ ○ ○ ○	

CPSIA information can be obtained
at www.ICGtesting.com
Printed in the USA
LVHW060531291222
736131LV00021B/287